Unfrocked and Unashamed

A Collection of Humorous Stories from the Courtroom

Manuel P. Scarmoutsos

PREMIUM PRESS AMERICA
NASHVILLE, TENNESSEE

Unfrocked and Unashamed by Manuel P. Scarmoutsos

Published by PREMIUM PRESS AMERICA

Copyright © 2003 Manuel P. Scarmoutsos

All rights reserved. No part of this book may be reproduced or transmitted in any form or by any means, electronic or mechanical, including photocopying, recording, or by any information storage and retrieval system, without prior written permission of the Publisher, except where permitted by law.

ISBN 1-887654-02-X
Library of Congress Catalog Number 2003115234

PREMIUM PRESS AMERICA gift books are available at special discounts for premiums, sales promotions, fund-raising, or educational use. For details contact the Publisher at P.O. Box 159015, Nashville, TN 37215, or phone toll free (800) 891-7323 or (615) 256-8484, or fax (615) 256-8624.

Web-site *www.premiumpressamerica.com*

Design by Armour&Armour, Nashville, Tennessee

First Edition 2004
1 2 3 4 5 6 7 8 9 10

This book is dedicated to my father, wife, children and grandchildren.

Acknowledgments

For years I have wanted to do this book, but I know that it could not have been possible without the assistance and encouragement of others.

First, I am indebted to my wife and my son, Peter, for their help, stimulation, and suggestions (some of which I rejected).

I am very thankful to John Cassady, my former client and friend, for his help in the cartooning, as well as his suggestions on doing the book right.

Many thanks to Wayne Emmons, Esquire, my friend and *sinadelfos* (Greek for "colleague"), for his valuable cautions and aid.

Lastly, many thanks to the various lawyers in Memphis who contributed many of the funny stories here.

Beware of Greeks Bearing Books

BY WAYNE EMMONS

Manuel Scarmoutsos—the first time ever I saw his face, I screamed. I was a brand-new member of the legal profession, and several of us—rookies and other young lawyers—had gathered at a restaurant to softly, tenderly, and secretly speak ill of judges and older lawyers, and to wistfully speak of other careers we should have considered.

Anyhow, we were in a grouse session when this slightly older lawyer walked up and began some streaming audio years before there was streaming audio.

This guy could really talk and had no lack of confidence. He was funny, talkative, astute, and quick of wit, and he laughed insanely at his own jokes.

It was Manuel Scarmoutsos.

He looked every bit like the big Greek he was, and he spewed forth inanities, jokes, and a veritable buffet of one-liners. In subsequent weeks as I came to know him better, I learned several things about him.

1. He over-married. Anyone who knows Georgia will testify to that on a stack of Bibles. The fact that he talked her into marriage speaks volumes of his powers of persuasion. Indeed, he could sell timeshare condos yet to be built on Mount Olympus in the village of Zeus himself.

2. He has never been low on self-confidence. I'm sure he's the only person on the planet who thinks that Georgia should be more grateful for getting him than him getting her. Psychiatrists call it delusional, out-of-control ego-inflation that should be treated with strong medicine.

3. He is an outstanding lawyer who is funny, knowledgeable, conscientious, talented, and compassionate.

4. He made me write #3 above—under threat of leaving me out of the book completely.

5. But, I've got to say honestly about the book . . . to quote Tony the Tiger, "It's grrrrreat!"

6. Now, I have done what I've promised you, Scarmoutsos, so deliver on your promise to me and keep me in your book. Otherwise, may the pigeons of the Parthenon drop large and many droppings on your head.

Humor

"A merry heart doeth good like a medicine..."
PROVERBS 17:22

HUMOR gives us smiles, laughter, and gaiety... HUMOR reveals the roses, and hides the thorns... HUMOR makes our burdens light and smooths the rough spots... HUMOR gives us the capacity to clarify the obscure, to simplify the complex, to deflate the pompous, to punish the arrogant and please the docile....

Regretfully, humor has often been in low repute among *over-serious* people who ban it from their hearts. This is as true today as it was yesterday of distrustful ones who refuse dosages of humor for their pessimism! They equate humor with buffoonery and think that humor devotees are silly fools unconcerned with problems of humanity.... I DENY THESE ALLEGATIONS AND RESENT THE ALLIGATORS!

HUMOR binds the wounds of those who suffer... wipes the tears from those who weep... and helps to heal the hurt of those whose hearts are broken....

LONG LIVE HUMOR!

Ouch!!!!

Alan Glenn is a member of the Tennessee Criminal Court of Appeals. Earlier in his career he was a lawyer in Civil Court as well as an assistant attorney general in Criminal Court in Memphis.

Justice Glenn is a quiet, polite person, rather shy, but handles his duties with dispatch and distinction. Thus, he seemed to be out of place as a prosecutor years ago because he was so nice to everyone.

One time, he was prosecuting a husband for assaulting his wife. It was alleged that he stabbed her in the head with a pair of scissors. When the wife took the stand, and after she testified as to her name and address, lawyer Alan asked, "Madam, on such and such a date, does anything stick in your mind?" It took minutes for the laughter to subside and lawyer Alan sought a place to hide.

Manuel P. Scarmoutsos

Somebody Throw Me a Rope, I'm Sinking!

Eugene C. Gaerig is another fine lawyer who has risen through the ranks to become an outstanding advocate. However, he is quick-witted and can be funny and entertaining. Many years ago he started out as an assistant attorney general prosecuting defendants in court.

He was prosecuting a death case one day. In all death cases, the state is required, among other matters, to prove the cause of death by competent medical testimony, usually a doctor licensed in the state. When that witness was on the stand, Gaerig's questions began like this:

"Doctor, are you licensed to practice medicine in Tennessee?"

"No."

"In Mississippi?"

"No."

"In Arkansas?"

"No."

"ANYWHERE?"

Judge Sylvanus Polk

Judge Sylvanus Polk was a probate court judge for many years in Memphis. Though basically fair, he was stern, caustic, and usually gave attorneys a difficult time in court. In addition to wills and estates, probate court was the forum to determine whether a person was competent to handle his own business affairs.

Lawyer Bill James had a client who was served with a summons to appear before Judge Polk for a hearing, but the legal papers did not mention competency, only charged Assault & Battery.

Jumping on the error, Bill said to the judge, "My client has NOT been properly served," and confidently sat down in his chair. Judge Polk looked at the client sitting in the second row, and, without batting an eye, said, "Consider him served."

Judge Marion Boyd

We Must Do Our Best

Federal Judge Marion Boyd—tall, proud, and very business-like—was a no-nonsense judge. Once, a bank robbery defendant had been found guilty. On the sentencing day, Judge Boyd said, "Sir, having been found guilty by the jury, I am going to sentence you to ten years in federal prison." Aghast, the defendant stated, "Judge, I don't think I can do that!" Without blinking an eye, Judge Boyd replied, "Well, sir, just do the best you can."

Weather Report

Wayne Emmons, a/k/a "Cousin Bubba," a local favorite lawyer, once said, "Don't take yourself too seriously: Remember the number of people at your funeral will be largely governed by the weather."

Wonderful and He Belongs to Me

Lawyer Glenn Sisson was representing a defendant who was pleading guilty before Judge Otis Higgs in Criminal Court. The judge was inquiring of the defendant to be sure the defendant understood his rights and what he was doing.

One of the questions was whether he had any complaints with his lawyer's representation. "Oh, your Honor, he is wonderful!" shouted the defendant. Judge Higgs could not resist, and calmly replied, "I have known Mr. Sisson for thirty years, and he is a good lawyer, but I don't know how wonderful he is!"

White Socks Suck!!!!

Most lawyers are skeptical about representing clients in other jurisdictions, especially in rural areas, since we all fear the "home cooking" that results often in the decisions.

Several years ago, I represented a young lady, Bonnie, in a post-divorce case set in Petersburg, Indiana. In the divorce, the judge awarded custody of the two small children to the father. After the divorce, Bonnie moved to Memphis, but she wanted to go back to court to regain custody of the children. I warned of the difficulties involved in rural Indiana, but she insisted.

We went to Petersburg, a small county seat. When out of town, I usually visit the local coffee shop where all the "important" locals hang out and just listen. There, I realized that "redneck" is an attitude not reserved to the South!

It was time for court! I knew I was in trouble when the judge entered the courtroom not wearing a robe. I knew I was in further trouble when I noticed the judge sported a crew cut, but what made me realize I was in deep trouble was when I saw the judge was wearing WHITE SOCKS!

(p.s. We not only lost the case, but the ex-husband and his attorney never appeared at the hearing!)

Help, Judge!

One of my earliest and best clients is Solon Tomlinson Jr. who recently retired from Northwest Airlines. When I first met him, he was employed by Southern Airlines, which became Republic Airlines and then Northwest. I handled his divorce.

He had a daughter from his divorce, but experienced great difficulty with his ex-wife concerning child visitation. We had to file post divorce petitions for contempt of court more than once. The judge was the late William O'Hearn.

At the first hearing she was represented by a lawyer, but at the second hearing she told the judge she could not afford a lawyer and represented herself. To our shock she prevailed at the second hearing. I think the judge felt sorry for her.

There was a need for a third hearing. Again, his ex-wife told the judge that she could not afford a lawyer, and I jumped up and said, "Please appoint her a lawyer, Judge, because she seems to do better without a lawyer!"

Politically Correct

Once I was in Juvenile Court with my client against his ex-wife. The judge was George Blancett (a former classmate of my wife at Humes High). During the proceedings, I referred to the ex-wife as "this little lady." I was polite, but Blancett looking down his glasses said, "That's not politically correct, Mr. Scarmoutsos." I rebutted, "It was good enough for Frank Glanker (top lawyer) for thirty-five years, it's good enough for me!"

It Ain't Me, Judge!

Years ago I was involved in an appeal from small claims court that came up in Judge John Wilson's court. The late Maurice McGhee represented a landlord, and I represented a tenant. The landlord sued for unpaid rent, and my client had a claim for set-off. It was a terrible case because the difference was like thirteen dollars.

When Judge Wilson realized that, he was furious. Grabbing his bald head with both hands, he exclaimed, "How did this case get here?" In my defense, I replied, "Don't look at me, Judge, McGhee's the one who appealed!"

Pick Out the Mean Judge!

Judge Charles O. McPherson followed Judge John W. Wilson in Division II of Circuit Court after Judge Wilson passed away. As I explained before, Judge Wilson was really stern on the bench, often snarling his face, which usually expressed his displeasure with either the lawyer or the case.

"Chuck" McPherson was not far behind as he, too, was often not a "happy camper" on the bench, or at least he appeared that way to some lawyers and some litigants. Off the bench, Judge McPherson was very friendly to all the lawyers.

It is customary to place portraits of former judges in the courtroom in which they served in the past. One day, an oil portrait of Judge Wilson was placed in Judge McPherson's court directly behind his chair. I entered the courtroom early one morning and saw the portrait and exclaimed to the court clerk, "I ain't coming in this room anymore!" The clerk asked why, and I added, "Because I am not going to look at *two* stern faces in the morning."

Judge Charles O. McPhearson
followed the late Judge John W. Wilson

Judge John W. Wilson

Need a Job?

Judge John Wilson served as circuit judge for many years in the 1950s until the '70s. Moderately qualified, he displayed his impatience with many lawyers, especially if the lawyer were unprepared in his mind. That was all right, but he was too verbally brutal more often than not. He earned many nicknames like, "Captain Nice," "Mr. Compassion," and "Jolly John." I got to know him better after he retired, and I found him to be shy and friendly.

One morning, a young, inexperienced lawyer was presenting his case poorly. I don't know, but it might have been his first case. Judge Wilson called him to approach the bench. Cupping his hands together around his semi-bald head and with gritted teeth, Judge Wilson asked him, "Have you ever considered another line of work?"

Judge Irving M. Strauch

Pardon My Back!

Judge Irving M. Strauch was one of the most brilliant judges ever to sit on the bench in Memphis. As a state trial judge, he presided over many types of cases including divorce, personal injury, contract disputes, workers' compensation, etc. Off the bench he was warm, friendly, and shy. On the bench he was always very serious to the extent that he appeared mad and impatient.

A story that has been confirmed by many lawyers is when lawyer Stanley Kline was before Judge Strauch one morning arguing a motion for his client. For some reason, Judge Strauch and Kline did not get along well. Right in the middle of Stanley's argument suddenly and without warning, Judge Strauch swirled his chair around facing the wall behind him. Astonished, Stanley asked, "Anything wrong, Judge?" Turning his head, Judge Strauch replied, "The Supreme Court said I have to listen to your argument. But it didn't say I had to look at you!"

Manuel P. Scarmoutsos

The "Keep Your Trash in Shelby County" Argument

Several years ago, a young lawyer called me at home on a Sunday evening, and asked me to appear in Bolivar, Tennessee, court the next morning to represent two young men on a burglary trial. He said it was an open-and-shut case since they were caught at the scene, etc. Lawyer Tom had to be in federal court the same morning. Another "freebie"!!!!!

So I got up early the next day, and travelled the seventy-five miles to Bolivar arriving at about 8:30 a.m. to meet my "clients." The trial began at 9:00 a.m. Sure enough, these two young black lads did not have a chance, as the proof was overwhelming. I did the best I could, but it was an impossible case for the defense. But, the fun was just beginning.

The summation (closing arguments) began at around 3:00 p.m. The presiding judge was Herman Reviere, from Ripley, Tennessee, a pleasant man who was anxious to conclude the case so he could make the long drive home. He was known for his anxiety and impatience.

The state argued first. The prosecutor, the late Preston Parks, a gentle, elderly gentleman, got up and said, "Ladies and gentlemen of the jury, you have got to punish these young boys from Shelby County (Memphis) who come up here and rob the good citizens!" He harped on that point and that point alone for at least fifteen minutes, waving the flag, etc., and finally sat down.

It was now my turn. I arose slowly and looked at the jury. "Ladies and gentlemen of the jury, I wish to speak with you only about what Mr. Parks told you. He said to punish these young men because they are from Shelby County. If that is your thinking, DO IT NOW" as I slammed my fist on the wooden rail facing the jury box. I continued, "Don't waste your time, the judge's time, our time, everybody's time!" Waving my finger back and forth, I added, "But, if that is your thinking, DON'T YOU DARE COME TO SHELBY COUNTY TOMORROW!" Well, it worked.

Judge Reviere was livid as the jury was out for almost three hours. When the jury returned, hopelessly deadlocked, it was close to 7:00 p.m. As a mistrial was declared, Judge Reviere gave me the worst stare, but I just shrugged my shoulders. "Just doing my job, Judge."

Manuel P. Scarmoutsos

Custer's Last Stand

A long time ago, I represented a man who ran a discount theater in Memphis that charged one dollar admission. In those days, discount theaters were common across the nation. They obtained film after the major theaters had run them for weeks. Their right to film was called "availability."

Columbia Pictures had produced a big hit called *Ghostbusters*. After *Ghostbusters* had made its run in Memphis for many weeks, it was supposed to be "available" to my client, who was thrilled since Christmas was but a few weeks away. However, Columbia advised my client that it had made a corporate decision not to allow discount theaters to run the film.

Whereupon, I filed a complaint for restraint of trade in federal court, as well as an immediate injunction to require that the film be made available to my client now!

The case landed in Judge Robert McRae's court; he was a liberal free spirit. I felt good that he would support the disadvantaged. I arrived in court with my client, and his main witness, another client: Charles Arendall, a successful business and sub-distributor for small theater owners in the Mid-South.

I looked across the counsel table and representing Columbia Pictures were three lawyers from Memphis (including now Federal Judge Jon McCalla), three lawyers for Columbia from the New Orleans office, two lawyers from California, and two corporate officers from California.

The first to speak was Judge McRae who looked at me and said, "Mr. Scarmoutsos, what have you got to say?"

Looking at the ten adversaries surrounding me, I gasped, "Now I know how General Custer felt!"

Judge Robert McRae

Manuel P. Scarmoutsos

"It's Eighteenth-Century Time"

Years ago, I represented a young man named Dan in Circuit Court Division VIII in a contested divorce case. He and his wife had two young daughters, probably then six and eight years old. The judge was the late William W. O'Hearn, a kindly, deeply religious man, extremely dedicated to his profession. In divorce matters, he usually leaned with the woman, especially if she was a mother.

In this case, the wife sued my client charging cruel and inhuman treatment. While the case was pending, my client suspected she was seeing another man, and thus he hired a private detective to spy on her. We then filed a cross-action alleging her misconduct.

The private eye testified that he posted himself outside her house for several evenings, and that an unknown male would arrive at her home from 6:00 to 6:30 P.M. about five to six times and leave her home about 8:00 P.M. In my mind, I thought those visits were for dinner only. However, since my client was seeking custody of his daughters, I was duty-bound to make hay with his suspicions. The judge was disturbed about this.

During the closing arguments I hit hard on the "dinner" visits. In response, my adversary, Blanchard Tual Jr. a prominent and rising attorney, attempting to soften my blows, said to the judge, "And besides, Judge, *this is the twentieth century!*" Well, lo and behold, the judge not only granted the husband his divorce, but awarded unto him the custody of the two daughters.

Later in the hallway, my friend Blanchard was visibly shaken. Hoping to cement our relationship, I said to Blanchard, "That was a wonderful closing argument you made, except for one point."

"What was that?" asked Blanchard. "Simple," I said, "*The judge lives in the eighteenth century!*"

Fantasy or Reality?

William Ray Ingram was a Judge in General Sessions back in the 1980s. While on the bench, he was known by most lawyers to be polite, sometimes humorous, but generally prosecution-minded. Johnny Pritchard, an active and successful lawyer in the courts, is one who knows his way around the system.

One day he represented a man charged with carrying a concealed weapon. The case was before Judge Ingram. Lawyer John filed a "motion to suppress" since there was a warrant question about whether the search was lawful. The two arresting officers gave obviously conflicting testimony about the search to an extent that neither was believable to all in attendance.

After the state rested, Lawyer John asked the judge to grant his motion to suppress. When the judge ruled, "Motion denied," Pritchard, in an astonished voice exclaimed, "Why, Judge?" And without batting an eye, the judge said, "The gun was in the car, wasn't it? Besides, we deal with reality in Division 9!"

Got the Wrong Charlie

Jury selection was seriously underway in Judge Arthur Bennett's courtroom on a high-profile, aggravated assault and child rape case. Lawyer Wayne Emmons, with white skin, white hair, and a white beard, was one of the prosecutors. Judge Bennett introduced the lawyers to the prospective jurors, and inquired as to whether any juror knew any of the lawyers. One juror stood up, pointed at Emmons, and said, "He looks familiar, but maybe it's because he looks so much like Charlie Pride."

The judge suppressed a laugh. Emmons stood up and said, "I bet he meant to say Charlie Rich, not Charlie Pride." "Oh yeah," said the juror, "Charlie Rich, not Charlie Pride!" It took a recess to get the court back to the serious business at hand.

Old Lawyer

Lawyer Glen Sisson tells the story about his client, an elderly Jewish lawyer in a nursing home, who had the following complaint:

"There's a man here who hasn't practiced medicine in over twenty years, and everybody calls him 'Doctor.'

"There's another man who hasn't been a choir director in over fifteen years, and everybody calls him 'Maestro.'

"I haven't had any sex in thirty years, and they call me, 'That screwing Jewish lawyer!'"

Pearl Harbor!!!!!

This case was reported in the local newspaper. Willard Dixon was a judge in General Sessions Civil Court many years ago. A Japanese-American was being sued for failure to pay his rent on time. He was found guilty, and Judge Dixon advised him that he had ten days to leave the premises. Lawyer Robert L. Dinkelspiel was in the courtroom when the defendant told the judge, "That's not fair, Judge." Answering, Judge Dixon said, "Pearl Harbor wasn't fair!"

This Boy is Honest!!!!!!

Edward Chandler, "Fast Eddie" to his friends, is a good lawyer with bountiful imagination in his approach to cases and peoples' rights. He is extremely loyal to clients and labors with vigor and dedication. Most of his practice has been in the criminal field, but he is adept with civil matters as well.

Once he was trying a DWI case, and as he was examining his client about his drinking, the client interrupted and said, "I was brain dead." Fast Eddie replied, "I don't understand." To Eddie's shock, his client started asking him a series of questions as if Eddie were the witness. It went like this:

"Do you drink?"

"Why, yes I do."

"Do you drink a lot?"

"Maybe, once and a while."

"Have you ever been brain dead?"

"... (pause) ... Not in a year."

Go—Stay—Or Do Both

An elderly judge in Criminal Court was going through his cases one morning to determine which cases were ready, which were not ready, and which needed a continuance. One lawyer said he was ready, but needed to go to another court for another announcement, to which the judge said, "You may leave the courtroom, or you may stay, or you may do both."

Educating the Young

Judge John Colton Sr. was a judge in Criminal Court during the 1970s and '80s. He was a master of the one-liners! Prior to being a judge, he practiced law for years. One day a man came into his office and said, "I got my arm broke in three places."

Lawyer Colton replied, "You have got to stay out of those places!"

UNFROCKED AND UNASHAMED

Judge John Colton Sr.

Welcome To the Courtroom???

Once while a criminal trial was in progress, a school teacher with her fifth grade class entered the courtroom on a field trip. The judge halted the proceedings and welcomed the class, and said, "I am the judge here, over here is the jury, and over there is John Smith, the prosecutor, and over there is William Jones, the attorney who represents the defendant. Behind Mr. Jones is I.R. Miller, who robbed the 7-11 store."

Check the Dewpoint

Judge Craig Hall is a part-time judge in Collierville, Tennessee, a suburb of Memphis. Craig practiced full-time law in Memphis. A cherubic fella, he is a capable, friendly lawyer, but can be tough when the need arises.

One day, lawyer Glen Sission represented an unsavory defendant in Collierville City Court who was charged with multiple serious charges. As the judge bound the defendant to the action of the grand jury, he said to the defendant, "Sir, as long as the dew sits on the grass in Collierville, you are not welcome *here*."

UNFROCKED and UNASHAMED

Judge Craig Hall

Manuel P. Scarmoutsos

**Judge James M. Tharp
Railroad Crossing Case
"The Prepared Witness"**

Any Further Questions?

James Tharp was a practicing attorney for many years before he assumed the bench as judge of Circuit Clerk III, and his service as a judge was a credit to the community. As a rule, it was a pleasure to advocate cases in his courtroom, as he treated lawyers and litigants with courtesy and patience.

He told a story about an example of a "prepared witness." It went like this. A railroad crossing case was tried in rural Tennessee. The plaintiff's lawyer saved his star witness, a ten-year-old country boy, for last. The plaintiff's lawyer, with great flourish, asked the boy, "What is your name?"

The immediate response was, "MY NAME IS JOHNNY JONES, THE WHISTLE WARN'T BLOWING, THE BELL WARN'T RINGIN', AND THERE WARN'T NOBODY KEEPING A PROPER LOOKOUT."

Making Law?

Judge Willard Dixon served as General Sessions judge for many years in Memphis. A portly, but friendly judge, he was often bored with hearing cases day after day, month after month and year after year. That was understandable, because most of the time, civil cases in General Sessions are usually boring in that most deal with bill collecting, rental defaults, etc.

One time, the late J.B. Cobb, an equally friendly lawyer, was trying a personal injury case, and there was an important point of law that J.B. was addressing, but found resistance from the judge. As J.B. was attempting to make his point, he said to the judge, "Don't you want to make some law in this case?" To which Judge Dixon replied, while looking at the clock on the wall, "All I want to make is retirement."

Thanks For the Help, Judge

Following a long and protracted divorce case, Judge James Tharp announced to the weeping wife, "Mrs. Jones, I am going to grant you the divorce, custody of your minor child, and one thousand dollars child support." They say the husband popped up and said, "That's mighty generous of you, Judge; I am going to chip in a few hundred dollars myself."

"God Tells Me What to Smoke!"

A no-nonsense, stern jurist, Judge William Williams, had before him a man charged with possession of marijuana. After he pled guilty, the man was on the witness stand seeking probation since it was his first offense. Chip Moore, a long-time assistant public defender, was attempting to ask the judge to suspend sentence.

All of a sudden, and without any prompting, the defendant spoke out and said, "Judge, I smoke marijuana because GOD told me to do so." Hearing that, Judge Williams said to the defendant, "Sir, look at me. . . . THIS GOD is telling you NOT to!!!"

Forgiveness, Yes... Probation, No!

Don Dino who was a prosecutor in the attorney general's office for years, retired and went into private practice representing many defendants in criminal cases.

One morning, after pleading his client guilty, he was seeking probation for his client. The presiding judge was Judge Arthur Bennett. It was well-known that Judge Bennett was active in his church, and sometimes quoted from Scripture. Knowing that, Don, in his summation to the court, stated, "Remember, Judge, even Jesus forgave the thief on the cross!"

Politely, the judge replied, "That's very true, but the thief didn't get probation!"

**Attorney Don Dino
and Judge Arthur Bennett**

Justice?????

Joseph Bearman was a delightful old timer who actively practiced law from the 1930s to the 1960s. His nephew, Leo Bearman Jr. and his grandson Steve Bearman are still practicing today. The Bearman name is a landmark in legal circles of Memphis and the state of Tennessee.

"Mr. Joe," as I called him, allowed me to share space in his office for five years in the 1960s. Intelligent, clever, sarcastic at times, respected, he was a delight to be around.

One morning, he was asked to sit as special judge in Criminal Court, which he did often in those days. As he walked through the courtroom en route to the judge's office, one of the lawyers sitting in the courtroom said, "Hi, Joe, are you going to dispense justice today?"

Without missing a beat, Mr. Joe answered from the corner of his mouth, "I am going to dispense with it!"

Life Before Death

One time, Jim Marty, a proficient lawyer in criminal matters, represented a man who was found guilty in a very terrible murder-plus case. The case was before Judge W. Williams.

At the day of sentencing, Judge Williams told the defendant, "On the charge of aggravated kidnaping, I am sentencing you to life without parole; on the charge of aggravated rape, I am sentencing you to life without parole; and on the charge of murder, I am remanding you to the warden of the state penitentiary, and that on a certain date you be taken to the electric chair where sufficient voltage be entered into your body until you are DEAD, DEAD, DEAD. Have you anything to say?"

In a squeaky, humbling voice, the Defendant asked, "Judge, can I do the "lifes" first?"

Manuel P. Scarmoutsos

"Marriage is like eating in a restaurant. . . . You think you like what you got, until you see what's at the next table."

"First the Verdict … Then the Evidence"

Some lawyers did not like Judge John Wilson, especially the younger ones. However, he had many friends, especially among such older lawyers as Leo Bearman Sr. who did not need the judge's help as he was one of the most outstanding lawyers in the state of Tennessee. However, he was not one to turn help down.

Many years ago, Jim Johnson (an All Southeastern Conference fullback from Vanderbilt University) was a new lawyer representing a plaintiff in Judge Wilson's Court. Mr. Bearman represented the defendant. The judge asked Johnson what the case was all about and what was his position.

The judge then asked the same question of Bearman, who also explained his position, but added, "Besides, I think the case should be dismissed." Judge Wilson then said, "I think so, too. CASE DISMISSED!"

(Those were the good ol' days.)

Manuel P. Scarmoutsos

How High is the Moon... How High is the Sky?

Eddie Peterson now practices civil law. For years, he was a prosecutor in the criminal courts in Memphis. During trials, he was known for his sarcasm during cross-examination of witnesses.

One time he was cross-examining an elderly man who was a key identification witness in a murder trial, and attempted to impeach or attack the witness' ability to see at night under a street lamp post. The question went like this:

"Isn't it true you wear glasses?"

"Yes."

"Isn't it true it was dark out there that night?"

"Yes."

"Isn't is true that you were about two hundred feet away?"

"Yes."

"Isn't it true you can't see that far at night?"

"I can see the moon, how far is that?"

"Stay Away From This Bat"

Lawyer Wayne Emmons, a/k/a "Cousin Bubba," had a client in Judge Williams' court years ago. It was a fairly serious case. A very reasonable plea offer was made by the D.A.'s office, which Emmons urged his client to accept. He explained to him in detail what could happen to him if he refused the offer—much more jail time—possibly a lengthy sentence, and that if he refused the plea to the lesser charge there would only be one choice left and that would be a jury trial. "You will have to go to bat."

Emmons told his client to sit in the courtroom and watch what happened while he went to other courts to handle some cases. He told his client that later in the day they would have to decide either to accept the plea to a reduced charge with time or just "go to bat before the judge and jury."

His client sat in court and watched the proceedings on other cases. Judge Williams was apparently in rare form, giving a stiff verdict of twenty years when a defendant had turned down a five-year plea bargain.

Wayne's client found him after seeing that and told him, "I want to take that plea bargain; I don't want to go before THIS BAT!"

"Hello, This is Captain Kirk!"

Irv Zeithlin is a quiet, friendly lawyer, who is known for handling tons of cases. Soft-spoken, he was always pleasant with everyone. He was so casual in his demeanor that his nickname was "Lightning Zeithlin."

Once Irv was arguing a motion in Circuit Court. Irv was not doing well in his opposition to the motion and became frustrated as his points were shut down by the late Judge William Leffler one after the other. As he stood at the counsel table, Irv was asked by Judge Leffler, "What do you have to say now, Mr. Zeithlin?"

Irv looked around and calmly reached into his jacket for his cell phone, held the cell phone to the side of his mouth and said, "Beam me up, Scotty!"

UNFROCKED AND UNASHAMED

**Judge Leffler
and Lawyer Irv Zeithlin**

Manuel P. Scarmoutsos

Arraignments
(AKA, Who is Your Mouthpiece?)

Judge William W. Williams served a long time as judge of Division III of the Criminal Court in Memphis. He also served as a former county attorney, and before then as an assistant attorney general. In all those positions, his reputation was that of sternness, often fair, and no-nonsense. There was little humor in his courtroom unless he did it.

They tell of an incident during arraignments when an elderly woman appeared before, and the questioning went like this:

Judge: "Do you have a lawyer?"

Lady: "I've got twelve children."

Judge: "One of them a lawyer?"

Judge William W. Williams

Judge "Jolly John" Wilson

Years ago, lawyer Jimmy Hicks, a quiet, slow-moving, but very effective advocate, was representing a client in Wilson's courtroom. The man was injured badly in an auto wreck, and his injury caused him to shake uncontrollably. There he sat in the second row, arms and legs shaking.

Judge Wilson blurted out, "Mr. Hicks, can't you get your client to stop shaking like that?"

Ole Jimmy, without looking up from his notes calmly answered, "That's why we are here, Judge."

Sayonara!

Judge William Williams was a no-nonsense, businesslike judge. One day, after a lawyer had pled his client guilty, the defendant raised his hand and said, "Can I say something, Judge?" The judge replied, "If it is anything but 'Goodbye', no!"

Judge Andrew Holmes

Before being elevated to the Tennessee Supreme Court, Judge Holmes was a trial court judge in Circuit Court of Tennessee at Memphis. A "throwback" to the "old school," he was a stern, deliberate jurist, tough, but generally fair.

Many years ago, two old-timers, Charley Morgan and Carlton Wilkes, represented the defendant and plaintiff in an automobile accident case. These two advocates fought bitterly in their clients' behalf. The court reporter in the case was Henry Waldauer, another old-timer, probably the dean of the court reporters then. However, Henry was tongue-tied when he spoke; except for the lawyers and Judge Holmes, no one at the trial knew that fact.

During the plaintiff's testimony, Mr. Wilkes asked him in cross-examination, "When were you married?" Unknown to all until then, the plaintiff was *also* tongue-tied. The plaintiff asked Mr. Wilkes to repeat the question. Where upon Mr. Wilkes said, "Mr. Court Reporter, would you please read the question?" Mr. Waldauer read the question in his tongue-tied way. The entire jury broke into loud and sustained laughter, and the plaintiff, thinking he was being made fun of, EXPLODED, shouting his anger to all to such an extent that Judge Holmes had to declare a mistrial.

False Witness

In another case in Judge Holmes' court, years ago, there was a contested divorce trial taking place. I do not recall the attorneys, but one of the lawyers called one of the witnesses to the stand. As is normal, witnesses wait in the hallway until called to the case.

The deputy went outside and called Mr. John Smith. Mr. Smith came into the courtroom and assumed the witness stand awaiting the questions from the attorney who called him.

The attorney inquired, "Do you know the parties in this case?" The answer was "No." The lawyer, dumbfounded, added, "Then why are you here?"

"I don't know either," said Mr. Smith, "I was just walking down the hallway going to the bathroom, when the deputy called my name."

UNFROCKED AND UNASHAMED

Poor Billy

One of the best lawyers I know is William H. Fisher, III. A really good person, Billy is most capable in his successful law practice. He is always well-prepared and "leaves no stones unturned," and if you are on the opposite side, you best be ready because he always is!

When Billy was a freshman lawyer years ago he appeared in Judge John Wilson's courtroom one Friday morning. The room was filled with dozens of lawyers, clients, and spectators.

When it was his turn, Billy arose and said, "Judge, this case was specially set. . . ." But he hardly got the words out of his mouth when "Jolly John" interrupted and shouted, "Mr. Fisher, motions are never SPECIALLY set in my courtroom." Whereupon the judge went into a loud and humiliating attack on this young lawyer to such extent that Billy sat down and forgot why he was there. (Judge Wilson enjoyed picking on some lawyers.)

After the dust settled, an elderly white-haired lawyer arose and said, "Your Honor, this motion was specially set this morning." The silence was deafening, and one could hear a pin drop.

Manuel P. Scarmoutsos

Judge William Leffler

The late Judge Leffler was one of the friendliest and most polite judges I have ever known. He was nice to everybody, probably because he possessed a genuine sense of humor, which he shared with all. Many years ago, I met the judge in the hallway of the courthouse, and he said to me, "Hi, Manuel, how are you doing?" I replied, "Hi, Bill, I made a five-dollar fee today and a small one!" Well, that broke him up, and for years thereafter, whenever our paths crossed, he would ask me about any five-dollar fees.

UNFROCKED AND UNASHAMED

**Judge Leffler and
Attorney Manuel Scarmoutsos**

Tell It to the Judge

I do not recall which court, but long ago, I was trying a divorce case. In those days, it was permissible to charge a man with insulting and cursing remarks, etc., as grounds for divorce. So I inquired of this lady on the witness stand what terrible and insulting things her husband called her. She puffed up and said, "Oh, he called me such names that are not fit for human ears." Then I said, "Just turn and tell them to the judge."

Feuding Lawyers

Don Owens Sr. and Wilbur Rulemand had a constant running feud whenever they met in court or socially. It was insult after insult, in good humor since they really liked each other.

One day, Wilbur was waiting in court to open, as were other attorneys. In walks Don Owens, and Wilbur spoke up in a loud voice, "Here comes my father!" Without missing a step, Owens replied, "I can't be his father; I'm married!"

Will Gerber

Will Gerber was the attorney general for Shelby County back in the 1940s-plus. Mr. Gerber, father of Hal and Marshall, both fine lawyers, was an aggressive and bombastic advocate of the "Old School" approach, and thus most effective for his time.

In court when prosecuting cases, he possessed a very loud and booming voice. In those days there were two divisions in criminal court, and the courtrooms were practically next door to each other.

They tell of a time that Mr. Gerber was trying a defendant in Division I so vigorously that he convicted that defendant and another defendant in Division II *at the same time!!!!!!!*

> "There is no such thing as small cases, only small people."
>
> Manuel P. Scarmoutsos

Deterrence

Two City Court judges were driving home in separate cars one day when they were both stopped by a motorcycle cop for speeding. The judges agreed that they would each try the other's case.

The first judge went to trial and was fined ten dollars. When they changed places, the second judge was shocked when he was fined fifteen dollars for the same offense. "That's a bit unfair," he said, "I fined you only ten dollars."

The first judge replied, "I know, but there is too much of this sort of thing going on, besides, *this is the second case we have had today!*"

Judge Wyeth Chandler

We Will Ask Judge Millie

Judge Chandler had a little terrier puppy (all of ten pounds) that he brought to court regularly and placed on the bench with him while trying cases. "Millie" was well disciplined, and only once in a great while did one hear a yelp. He was devoted to "Millie."

On Motion Day, another lawyer and I were arguing on a legal point, and we were all confused, including the judge, as how to resolve the issues. The judge appearing disgusted exclaimed, "I don't know what to do with this motion!" Seeking closure, I replied, "Well, just ask "Millie."

(p.s. I lost the motion.)

Dying To Be Lying

Exasperated after listening to a two-week trial where it was most obvious that many witnesses testified untruthfully, Judge McPhearson announced, "To quote a famous English statesman, 'Never in the course of human events have so many lied to accomplish so little!'"

Older is Better

Tom Pera is a very friendly, decent lawyer who, in his many years of practice, is well-known for his concern for his clients.

One morning he appeared with his client before Judge John Colton Sr. His client was very elderly, and wanted that known to the judge for whatever sympathy he could get.

As he sat behind his lawyer in the second row, he kept pulling on Tom's coat and saying, "Tell him how old I am . . . tell him how old I am." Exasperated, Tom exclaimed, "Hell, he's older than you!"

Attorney Thomas Pera

Manuel P. Scarmoutsos

"Spineless Wonder"

Former Judge Wyeth Chandler, a former city councilman and a former mayor, was without doubt one of the most colorful judges in the history of Memphis. He was a people person with a storied past. Lawyers enjoyed his courtroom because he moved cases quickly, often with vigor, and usually made the right decisions.

One day, lawyer Lillian "Noopy" Dykes was representing a lady in a hotly contested divorce case. The defendant was a doctor, and his evil conduct, according to the evidence, displeased Chandler immensely. When the judge finally ruled in the case, he said, "Sir, you are a spineless wonder, and I don't believe you would show up in an X-ray."

He Thinks Highly of You Too, Judge

William Hackett served as a judge in General Sessions Court in Memphis during the 1980s and '90s. He was usually polite to the public, but often "testy" with many lawyers. Lawyer Jim Marty had a case scheduled for trial in Hackett's court. Jim had a conflict that morning; because he was going to be a little late, he sent an associate over to tell Judge Hackett about the problem.

When the situation was explained to Judge Hackett, the judge shouted out, "I don't give a damn where Mr. Marty is, or what he is doing!" The associate quietly and politely replied, "That's exactly what he said about you."

I've Changed My Mind, Judge

Charles O. McPherson was a no-nonsense judge. Once, an ex-husband was summoned to court for not paying his child support in a timely manner. The ex-wife's attorney questioned the ex-husband, "Did you not tell your former wife on the telephone the other night that you were not going to give her one cent regardless of what the judge said?"

Meekly, the ex-husband looked at the judge's piercing eyes, and replied, "Yes, I did, but I don't feel that way this morning."

Everyone's a Comedian

Judge Arthur Facquin was a Criminal Court judge for a number of years back in the 1960s and '70s. One day he was trying a case in which the defendant was charged with murder and rape. This same defendant had already received the death penalty in a prior murder case.

This defendant was found guilty in both the murder and rape cases. The judge sentenced him to life in the first case and death in the second case. Then he ran the cases consecutively with the death sentence he had from the prior trial.

The defendant's lawyer could not resist, and said, "Obviously Your Honor believes in life after death!"

Manuel P. Scarmoutsos

Let's All Chip In For the War

Lawyer Bill Monroe was representing three "dancers" from a topless club being prosecuted for lewd conduct. The opposition wished to take the depositions of one of the dancers. At the deposition, the young lady was very forthright in her answers, seeking to cooperate as best she could. This took place during the Iraq War during the early 1990s. The opposing lawyer asked her what she charged her customers.

The dancer replied, "Well, three dollars for a table dance, and five dollars for a lap dance." She paused and added, "But, now we cut our prices to help the war effort!"

UNFROCKED AND UNASHAMED

The Deposition

Sheriff Buford Pusser... Walking Short

Back in the spring of 1976, I represented W.R. Morris, who wrote the book *The 12th of August*, a story about Sheriff Buford Pusser of "Walking Tall" fame. The suit was for breach of contract between Morris and Pusser. The trial lasted four days, and it was tried in Pusser's home area, Selmer, Tennessee.

Before the trial began, the sheriff was killed in an automobile accident, so the case was adjusted against the estate of Pusser, which made the trial atmosphere rather uncomfortable since Pusser was a local hero.

One of the newspaper reporters covering the case was Jerry Thompson of *The Tennessean*, a leading Nashville newspaper. There were many highlights of the case, but the following is an exact excerpt from his article on May 7, 1976:

"During one point in the testimony yesterday, while Morris's attorney, Manuel P. Scarmoutsos, was examining Morris, he was attempting to elicit testimony from Morris that Pusser had made threats and was a violent man. Gordon immediately jumped to his feet to object and Scarmoutsos started to ask him the question again. 'I was going to ask him,' Scarmoutsos said just before a flash of lighting illuminated the courtroom followed by a shattering clap of thunder that rattled the windows. Scarmoutsos looking toward the ceiling said, 'Maybe I'd better not ask the question.' That brought the whole courtroom to laughter...."

It's Me, It's Me, Cory B.

Years ago, the Supreme Court ruled that it was permissible for lawyers to advertise within certain limits. Not all lawyers advertise, but there are a substantial number that do. Some of the ads are befitting, and some are not befitting. In Memphis, probably one of the most-known advertising lawyers is Cory B. Trotz. He is everywhere: TV, radio, and even some billboards. Many do not need lawyers, but anyone who watches TV knows about Cory B. Trotz.

Cory, a delightful young man, has his office on the twenty-fifth floor of Clark Tower. My office is on the twenty-eighth floor. On the thirty-third floor is the Summit Club, a private club for dining. One morning, I entered the elevator on the ground floor with about eight to nine elderly ladies dressed in their finest, hats, furs, etc., who were in route to the Club for the Ladies Luncheon. Last entered Cory B. Trotz, and when he saw me there he cringed, cupping his hands around his head fearing what was coming. I turned to this complete stranger, a nice little lady with silver blue hair, and said, "Madam, my lawyer is Cory B. Trotz."

She said, "Really?" and I replied, "Yes, he got my check *before* the accident happened!"

"It pays to advertise…"
Attorney Cory B. Trotz

James W. McDonnell Jr.

Jim McDonnell Jr. now retired, was one of the finest and best prepared lawyers in Memphis. Somewhat outwardly "stiff," he was all business as a vigorous and serious adversary.

Many years ago, late 1960s, I represented a William Phansteill in a medical malpractice case against the late Dr. Aden Barlow. It appeared that Dr. Barlow had performed a vasectomy on my client, and unfortunately, Dr. Barlow had mistakenly severed a vein in my client's scrotum, to such an extent that the scrotum was inflamed to the size of an extra-large grapefruit. One can imagine Mr. Phansteill's excruciating pain!

As part of his preparation for trial, lawyer Jim set depositions for Mr. and Mrs. Phansteill. The court reporter was Vern Short, an equally serious and "stiff" professional.

Mrs. Phansteill was a good ol' country gal who always spoke her mind. As lawyer Jim was examining her about her husband's pain, and what she observed, etc., he kept referring to the scrotum this and the scrotum that, when Mrs. Phansteill interrupted him and asked, "Mr. McDonnell, can I ask a question?" "Of course," Jim replied. Cupping her hands and holding them high, she inquired, "When you say the scrotum, do you mean the balls?" The court reporter fell on his machine, I broke out in laughter, and flustered lawyer Jim said softly, "Yes."

Thereafter for years, whenever I saw the court reporter in passing, I cupped my hands and we would break into laughter.

James W. McDonnell Jr.

Manuel P. Scarmoutsos

Hello!

J udge Wyeth Chandler was unpredictable. One day, during a trial, the water pitcher at the counsel table was empty and the clients and lawyers needed immediate refreshment. A recess was declared, and Judge Chandler took the water pitcher to the water fountain in the hallway, but the fountain did not work. With the two lawyers in tow, he went to the restroom and tried to put the pitcher under the cold water faucet, but the pitcher would not work. As the lawyers gasped, Chandler put the pitcher in the commode, and filled it with the cold water. Pleased with his ingenuity, he said, "They will never know!"

UNFROCKED AND UNASHAMED

Judge Wyeth Chandler

Loved By Many... Feared By More

Chancellor Charles Rond served in Part III of the Chancery Court of Shelby County, Tennessee, for many years. A former prosecutor from the "old school," he was courteous, firm, business-like, yet possessed a very dry sense of humor. He was loved by many, but feared by many more.

I asked him once why some lawyers sit in their chairs when questioning witnesses and others stand when questioning witnesses, to which he answered:

"Sometimes they sit, sometimes they stand, and sometimes they lie!"

Chancellor Charles Rond

Manuel P. Scarmoutsos

The new lawyer

Believe Me, I Know What I'm Talking About... Don't I?

A new young lawyer had just opened his office. He saw someone approaching his door and said to himself that he must impress him... it may be his first client. So he picked up the telephone and said, "No, I'm sorry, I can not take your case even for a ten thousand dollar retainer fee. I'm too busy." He then turned to the man, saying, "What can I do for you?" The man replied, "Nothing really, I'm from BellSouth, and just came by to connect your telephone."

* * *

When I first started practicing law, I received a telephone call from a client in jail about a problem he had. I said to him, "They can't put you in jail for that!"

"Oh yeah, where do you think I am calling from, the public library?"

First the Proof... Then the Verdict

Years ago there was a lovable old-timer who was typical of those "from the old school." As criminal court judge, he had thousands of defendants appear before him during his career.

One morning, prosecutor Jim Garts, now a successful civil attorney, was about to begin a case against two defendants. The judge called Garts up to the bench, and whispered, "What should we do with these, general?" Garts replied, "Don't you think we should listen to the proof first?"

To which the judge said, "That's a good idea."

Nit' Picking?

Back in the 1950s, '60s, and '70s, there was a most colorful "ole timer" named W.C. Rogers who officed in the Exchange Building with many fellow lawyers. W.C., completely bald, was a rather cranky old fella, who asked for none, but gave no quarter in the pursuit of his cases. He was learned in the law, and a fierce adversary. He was devoted to his clients, and often would appeal cases even if he had to pay the costs himself if he felt the trial judge was wrong. He feared no one!

One day he was arguing a motion in Judge John W. Wilson's court. Wilson, not necessarily a friend of Mr. Rogers, proceeded to rule against the motion, and when he finished, Mr. Rogers pointed to the court reporter and said, "Let the record reflect that the trial judge was picking his nose while overruling my motion!"

"Nit Picking"
Judge John W. Wilson

Judge Joe Brown

Judge Joe Brown, presently of TV fame, served for several years as trial judge in Division IX of Criminal Court in Memphis. Then and now, Judge Brown was colorful and controversial, especially to the prosecution, since he was not a "yes man" to the prosecution.

One day, lawyer Brett Stein was trying a case in Judge Brown's Court. The trial recessed for the day. However, it was late, past 7:00 p.m. In the courtroom, Stein is loud and aggressive in his version of "the pursuit of justice," but at heart he is timid.

Seeing how dark and gloomy it was outside, Stein said to Judge Brown, "Gee, Judge, I'm afraid to go to my car outside since it is so dark, and you know how it is after dark downtown."

"Don't worry, Brett, I'll walk with you and I'm packing HEAT!"

Judge Joe B. Brown

Comma, Colon, or Semi-Colon

Sam Goldberger, a delightful "old timer," for many years was known during his extended career as "The King of Continuances" in Criminal Court. He made requests for continuances a fine art. The judges were both skeptical and amused by his efforts.

On one occasion he appeared before Judge John Colton Sr. and asked for a continuance on a case already put off four times. When the judge asked him the basis for a fifth continuance, he told him that he was going to have a serious operation. John Colton inquired, "What is the nature of the operation?"

Lawyer Sam stated, "I don't know the technical term for my operation, but my doctors tell me that when they're finished with me, my colon will be a semi-colon."

Kill Me, Kill Me, Please Kill Me

William E. Friedman is one of the better lawyers in Memphis. A sole practitioner for years, he is a tireless worker in preparing his cases and leaves nothing unattended before he goes to court. The rap on him is that he talks endlessly, not only in the presentation of his case, but even when he meets you on the street for small talk. However, he is truly a nice person.

One Friday, I and eight to nine lawyers were awaiting our turn to present certain motions for the court's consideration. The judge was the late William O'Hearn, a very polite and kindly man. When my motion was called, I went to the counsel table and stood with my hands on the table, head down, shaking back and forth. Judge O'Hearn, concerned "Anything wrong, Mr. Scarmoutsos?" I looked up and said, "Judge, I am so thankful you called my motion ahead of Mr. Friedman's, since had you not, I would have cut my wrists." Everybody, including the judge broke into laughter as Willie jumped up and announced, "I'm going to subpoena all of you to my slander trial!" (We are still friends.)

Manuel P. Scarmoutsos

Control Your Client... Even If You Have To Deck Him

I began practicing law in late 1960. The first year was uneventful. Business was slow, as I had not yet established client relationships.

The first contested case I had was in Circuit Court before Judge John W. Wilson. It was a bench trial (without a jury). Assisting me was my partner, Jimmie McIntyre. We represented this man against Sears Roebuck Co. over a roof repair matter. Our client was a quiet unassuming Italian-American chap named John.

When Judge Wilson announced his decision in favor of Sears, suddenly and without any warning, up jumped John shouting, "I knew it! I knew it! I knew I couldn't get a fair trial." John was so disruptive, that the judge summoned his court deputy for help. The deputy put a full nelson hold on John, dragging him to the door. When they reached the door, John screamed at the top of his voice to the judge, "YOU BASTARD!" Throughout all of his commotion, Jimmie and I sat motionless in our chairs ... we didn't know if this was routine behavior.

As John and the deputy struggled, they bumped against the courtroom door, and the antique ornamental glass in the door crashed onto the granite floor, making the loudest of noises, which brought dozens of deputies to the courtroom. As several deputies held the struggling John, Judge Wilson sentenced him to three days in jail.

Smirking, Judge Wilson called me up to his bench, and said, "Did you know this was going to happen?" The only reply I could think of was, "Well, I thought he was a little excitable."

Pay Attention, Glenn!

Many years ago, Chancellor Rond taught a class at the old University of Memphis night law school. One of his students was Glenn Sission, a busy and very likable lawyer. When Glenn passed the bar exam, he was introduced in open court in Rond's courtroom. Hard to miss: Glenn is as bald as a cue ball.

The Chancellor recognized his former student and told all the lawyers in his courtroom, "I remember this young man who always paid attention." A week later, Glenn entered an order in Rond's Court for the senior partner of his firm. Glenn was asked a question about the order that Glenn could not answer. Rond responded, "That's the problem with you; you don't pay attention!"

Manuel P. Scarmoutsos

How About the Tickets for Opryland?

Years ago, lawyer Louis Todd was defending a man who bought a boat and trailer from a marine supply store in Memphis, and was planning to take it to Nashville on one of the area lakes and do some sightseeing in Nashville.

As the plaintiff was towing the trailer, for some unexplained reason, the boat split in two causing the trailer to leave the highway and crash. The plaintiff claimed his damages were (1.) value of the boat, (2.) cost of the trailer, (3.) his gas to/from Nashville, (4.) his meals, (5.) hotel bills, and (6.) two tickets to Opryland.

The defense was that the splitting of the boat was a factory defect and not related to the marine supply company, which was strictly the middleman in the process. Judge Hackett said, "Judgment for the plaintiff, and I am going to give him the value of the boat, trailer, his meals, gas for the trip, and the hotel bill. Anything else, gentlemen?"

Lawyer Todd, reeling from the shocking decision, shouted, "Yeah, Judge, you forgot the two damn tickets to Opryland," as the courtroom broke into laughter.

Judge Bailey Brown

Judge Brown was a long-time federal judge in Memphis, as well as in Cincinnati for years. One day in court, while he was hearing what appeared to be an obviously frivolous lawsuit, he was heard to comment, "This country has become to be so litigious that it is going to come a time, when at Christmas, a husband is going to give his wife a lawsuit of her choice!"

Warren Miller

Lawyer Miller tells of a time when he was in Criminal Court waiting his turn to present his client's case. Ahead of him was an assault and battery case wherein a man and a woman were involved in a very heated fight. In fact, the man was alleged to have cut the woman with a knife.

In the cross-examination, the attorney for the defendant inquired of the victim, "Ms. Jones, I understand you were cut in the fracas?"

"No, sir," replied Ms. Jones. "It was just above the fracas."

Manuel P. Scarmoutsos

Career Advice

Lawyer Patrick Arnoult was a young lawyer once, appearing in Chancellor Rond's court for the first time. Pat had been appointed by the court as guardian *ad litem*, and presented his report to the court and requested the required fee for his services.

The court asked what amount he was requesting, and lawyer Pat replied, "Well, Your Honor, I have two dollars in costs, and I spent five hours of time at one hundred dollars per hour."

To which the Chancellor replied, "If you want to be paid by the hour, go be a plumber."

* * *

Lawyer Patrick had another case in Chancellor Rond's court in which a brother was suing his sister over property left by their recently deceased mother. It was hotly contested, and not a pleasant scene. As the case finally concluded, the chancellor made the following comment, "This is a dispute between a brother and a sister, who could not get the coins off their mother's eyelids before closing the coffin."

Swift Justice!

There was a City Court judge years ago in the 1960s and '70s who was indeed very colorful, but well-liked by so many. He was most practical in the handling of cases. Back then City Court met at night as well as the morning and afternoon sessions.

One night, before coming on the bench, this judge peeked through his office door and noticed a packed courtroom, hundreds or more waiting for their cases. The judge summoned his court officer, and told him to bring somebody from the street to appear as *first* defendant for trial.

Sure enough, the officer found a "homeless" soul to participate. After court convened, the judge announced in a loud voice to the homeless "defendant," "Sir, after a lengthy trial, I find you guilty and sentence you to twenty years in jail." (Then, the maximum penalty in City Court was a fifty dollar fine and ten days in jail.) The courtroom was stunned. As the "defendant" was taken away, a recess was called and EVERYBODY rushed to the prosecutor and pled guilty.

When the courtroom cleared, the judge called the "defendant" into the courtroom and handed him a hundred dollars. "This is for your trouble."

Moon Over McCartie

Public defendant Chip Moore represented a man in Judge McCartie's courtroom who was found guilty in a criminal case. At the motion for new trial hearing, Judge McCartie gave Chip and his client a very difficult time, and he finally ruled against the motion.

The defendant had taken all of the abuse he wanted from the judge, so he unzipped his pants and exposed his well-endowed manhood to the judge. He then turned around, lowered his trousers, and MOONED the judge. The courtroom exploded with laughter, except for the judge, as the defendant was escorted to jail. The assistant attorney general, Phyllis Gardner, still wide-eyed, was heard to say, "Well, he certainly had something to be proud about!"

"Moon" over McCartie

Judge Ray Churchill
"Democracy in Action…"

Democracy in Action

Many years ago, during Night Court, Judge Ray Churchill was faced with an extremely long docket. He and prosecutor Jog Tagg Jr. were becoming exhausted and it was getting late. As they neared the end of the docket, the judge had a particular case that was confusing.

He turned to the audience, to the shock of all including the prosecutor, and stated, "How many people think the defendant is guilty?" A few said, "Guilty."

"How many people think he is not guilty?" Most of the audience shouted "not guilty." The judge said, "CASE DISMISSED."

So!

There once was a judge in Criminal Court in Memphis who had an infamous reputation for being verbally abusive toward defendants in his court, especially when they were seeking a public defender claiming they were without funds. He believed everyone could have a job if he or she wanted to.

One morning, a poor soul seeking a public defender appeared before that judge. Under one of his arms he was leaning on a crutch. When he requested a free lawyer, the judge asked why he was not working. The man stated, "Can't, Judge, I only have one leg and one arm," and showed there were indeed two missing limbs. The judge shouted back, "SO!"

Got a Short Witness?

Lawyer Wayne Emmons, an outstanding advocate for people, is resourceful and unique, yet possesses a keen sense of humor when necessary.

For several years he was the prosecutor in Dyersburg, Tennessee, a community just seventy miles north of Memphis. He was trying a jury case before Judge Joe Riley, and it was near recess time for lunch. The judge stated, "Mr. Emmons, we have about fifteen minutes to go before lunch. Do you have a short witness?"

Lawyer Wayne couldn't resist and answered, "Well, Judge, I have one in the hall about five foot three inches. Is that short enough?"

Garland Draper

About forty years ago, a group of elderly lawyers were gathered in the Tennessee Club playing gin. It was a daily ritual around 5:00 p.m. for these "old timers" when the day's work was done. Someone rushed into the Club and announced that twenty-eight "ladies of the evening" were arrested, and were set for Night City Court, and that they were in need of some free lawyers to represent them.

Garland Draper, the "Dean" of the "old timers," stood, threw his cards down, and said, "Fellas, let's go down to court and help these young ladies!" Another lawyer got up and said, "You mean act as *amicus curia*?"

"No," blurted Garland, "*Amicus whorei!*"

Mom...Please Sit Down

Lawyer Jim Marty's mother became a close friend of a rather wealthy lady in Memphis. This lady lived in a large home complete with expensive antiques, china, silverware, etc. Her daughter married a young man, and the couple moved into a small cottage behind the large house. Because they needed more room, the couple moved into the large house, and the wealthy lady moved into the cottage.

However, shortly after that, the wealthy lady discovered that the couple was selling many of the expensive antiques, etc., in the home. Because of her close friendship with Marty's mother, she employed Jim to file suit to recover her property. The case was tried in General Sessions Court before Judge Morgan Fowler. Marty's mother insisted on attending the trial to support her friend of many years. During the trial, the wealthy lady's daughter said that her mother gave her the items in dispute.

Suddenly, Marty's mother jumped up from the audience and yelled, "That is a damn lie!" The stunned judge asked, "Who was that woman?"

Lawyer Marty answered, "That was no woman, Judge, that was my mother!!!"

Manuel P. Scarmoutsos

You Put Them To Sleep— You Wake Them!

Lawyer Hunter Lane Jr. was in the process of trying a fire loss case in federal court, and his adversary was Gary Smith, a most successful attorney who has tried many cases, usually as counsel for the insurance companies. It was a hot summer day, and the air conditioning was not working. The heat was unbearable.

Nevertheless, lawyer Smith was using a "full court press" attack from beginning to end attempting to discredit Lane's witnesses. As the oppressive heat got to the jury, one by one they began to nod off to sleep.

Smith asked for a quick recess; outside the presence of the jury, he and Lane approached the judge at his bench seeking a wakeup call from the judge. Smith asked the visiting judge from Detroit if he would arouse the sleeping jurors. The judge barked, "You wake them up, Mr. Smith, you put them to sleep!"

Hunter Lane Jr.

Manuel P. Scarmoutsos

"Jury Selection"
Ron and Nancy Guy

Put Some Clothes on Your Ugly Self

Ron and Nancy Guy have been friends of ours for many years. About twenty-five or thirty years ago, they were living with their two daughters in a condo at Bavarian Village in Germantown. Our home was just a few blocks away. One hot summer afternoon in July, they invited us with our young children to come over and share the swimming pool. So we put on our bathing suits, jumped in the car, and drove over to their pool. We had a wonderful time, and repeated it the following week. Unfortunately, the Guys moved from Bavarian Village after that and we lost contact for awhile.

A year or two later, I was about to begin a trial in criminal court. To my surprise, on the prospective jury was Nancy Guy. I don't think she recognized me. During the jury examination, the prosecutor asked the members of the prospective jury if anyone knew any of the lawyers in this case. Looking at me, Nancy put her hand to her mouth and said, "I think I know him, but I don't recognize him with his clothes on!"

Manuel P. Scarmoutsos

Who Done It

Ray Churchill was one of the sitting judges in the City Court of Memphis, Tennessee, during the 1960s and '70s. There were many judges in City Court in those days, but without question he was the most colorful. He was a trial lawyer for years, so when he assumed the bench he was considerably older than most lawyers. Slightly rotund, he was often bombastic and sometimes rude in his rulings, but he had a sense of humor.

As a lawyer and as a judge, he was known for championing the cause of the "underdog" because he felt government had a duty to prove one guilty of a law violation. He was definitely not a "rubber stamp."

Churchill's usual prosecutor was Joe Tagg Jr. Their confrontations were legendary. One time, there were multiple defendants charged with a city ordinance violation. The hearing went on for a very long time; at the end, Judge Churchill said, "I'm confused with the evidence and do not know whom to fine." To which Tagg shouted, "Fine them all, Judge, then you know you got the right one!"

Judge James E. Swearengen

Clarence Bowen was the court clerk in Judge Swearengen's courtroom for years. He told of a story once, when the air conditioning was not working during a jury trial and the windows were open so that a breeze could cool the courtroom.

Just then a wasp appeared and began circling around the courtroom and especially around the jury. Judge Swearengen quickly said to the courtroom deputy sheriff, "Take care of that wasp!" The deputy, an old timer, responded, "What do you want me to do Judge, shoot him?"

(P.S. The deputy was not in court the next day.)

Manuel P. Scarmoutsos

What Else You Gonna Do When Your Mama Told You To Be Courteous To Naked Women?

Attorney Philip Walker tells about observing a trial in General Sessions Criminal Court. The judge was Anthony Johnson. It appears a topless dancer was charged with open lewdness in doing a table dance at a club. The police officer was testifying about what the dancer was doing.

The officer said, "The dancer was parading around this man seated at a table, and placed one of her breasts in the man's mouth." Pouncing on the opportunity, the prosecutor interrupted, "And what did the man do?" The officer said, "He seemed to be enjoying it."

"He seemed to be enjoying it…"

Screaming for Justice!

Another time, a man was charged with an offense, and in the concluding summation, prosecutor Tagg exclaimed, "Judge, the people are screaming for justice." Judge Churchill rose from his bench, looked across the crowded courtroom, and said," I don't see or hear anybody screaming."

Judge Ray Churchill

Enough is Enough!!!!!!

A man rushed into his favorite bar, and shouted, "My lawyer passed away... my lawyer passed away... my lawyer passed away!" The bartender responded, "You said it three times." The man said, "I know, but I just love to hear it!"

How to Salute a Judge

City Court Judge Ray Churchill served Memphis for many years. A defendant was before the judge on the charge of disorderly conduct, and the charge was by a Memphis police officer, who claimed that the defendant gave him "the finger."

The hearing was short, but heated. Always innovative, the judge ruled, "I find that giving 'the finger' is a form of freedom of speech, and not disorderly conduct. This case is dismissed."

Frustrated, the police officer began to leave the courtroom and as he neared the exit, he hollered out to the judge, "Your Honor, may I address the court?" Churchill said yes. Whereupon the officer gave the judge "the finger."

Manuel P. Scarmoutsos

Judge John Colton Jr.

Judge Colton Jr. is the son of the late Judge Colton Sr. Like his father, Judge John Colton Jr. is polite and well-liked. Soft-spoken even as a lawyer, he brought to the bench an easy-going approach, but he could be stern when needed. He is not without a sense of humor, and from time to time liked to tease lawyers.

One day, a young lawyer, Steve Sauer, probably six feet tall, was addressing the court as Judge Colton, without batting an eye, said, "You know, I don't like tall lawyers." Sauer continued speaking, lowering his body until Judge Colton granted his request.

Judge John Colton Jr.

Manuel P. Scarmoutsos

A "Tittylating" Performance

Lawyer Hunter Lane Jr. likes to tell about one of his favorite cases he tried in City Court. The defendant was a twenty-three-year-old mother of three from Mississippi, about six feet tall with the body of a centerfold. She was charged by the ever-vigilant vice squad with "indecent

Hunter Lane Jr.

exposure and lewd and lascivious behavior" based on her performance as an "exotic dancer" (as distinguished from a stripper) at a grungy beer joint called the Islander, a favorite with the shift workers who worked at the various nearby industries. His client "Betty Lou" had her three children placed at a daycare center while their mother "tittylated" the horny shift. Her moves were stiff and amateurish except for an occasional weak pelvic thrust and wiggle of her well-toned buns.

The case was set in Judge Ray Churchill's courtroom. Betty Lou's overriding anxiety was that her husband, an iron worker employed in Mississippi, would learn of her secret since he worked the 3-11 p.m. shift, and the deception was working well.

The primary basis of the vice squad's charges was not her dance style, but her costume, which consisted of the usual pasties and tassels attached to her ample breasts, a bikini bottom, and high-heeled shoes. The celebrated Judge Churchill's fame was derived from his disdainful attitude toward all police witnesses. He was one of first local judges to question their credibility and insist on adequate proof from them to establish the defendant's guilt beyond a reasonable doubt.

The confident prosecutor put on the arresting officers and closed his proof with the proffer of several 8x10 glossy photos of Betty Lou in her skimpy costume. Lawyer Lane called the vice squad captain, who had to admit that there was not a city ordinance which defined "indecent, lewd and lascivious conduct." He admitted further that the "standards" would change from time to time without notice to the dancers.

The judge was becoming more and more agitated, especially when he glanced at the glossy photos. After a long pause, the great jurist grandly announced, "Hell, I've seen more skin than this in *The National Geographic*. CASE DISMISSED!"

Would You Like to be Judge for a Day?

In the past, lawyers were allowed to substitute in state trial courts for judges whenever judges were ill or had to "tend to some personal business." One day, Judge Terry L. Lafferty asked me to handle his docket for the day because the docket was only guilty pleas and arraignments . . . no trials.

That day, an elderly, kindly old lady appeared before me to request a public defender. I had to question her to determine if she qualified for a free lawyer. The questioning went like this:

Me: "Are you employed?"

Lady: "No, Your Honor, I am seventy-four years old."

Me: "Do you have any bank accounts?"

Lady: "No, Your Honor."

Me: "Do you own an automobile?"

Lady: "No, Your Honor, can't see to drive anyway . . . even if I could see, I ain't got nowhere to go."

Me: "Do you own a Picassos, Van Goghs, or Rembrandts?"

Lady: "Any what?"

Me: "Paintings . . . works of art!"

Lady: "I think I still got a couple of them paint-by-number deals from K-Mart . . . an elephant and a couple of tigers."

Me: "I think you qualify for a free lawyer."

(The prosecutor, Phyliss Gardner, just dropped her head!)

Pay the Fine!

At least twenty years ago, I had an elderly black gentleman for a client. I really liked Mr. Seymore, who was a very gentle soul. We had a few cases together over the years, and we established a nice relationship, as he would call me from time to time just to chat. He was genuine.

One hot summer afternoon, Mr. Seymore, then about eighty-five years old, had an argument with his eighty-year-old girlfriend out in the front yard. All they were doing was yelling at each other, which many old people do. But the neighbors thought it was serious and called the police. When the "boys in blue" arrived, probably two rookies, they searched Mr. Seymore and found a very small pistol in his pocket, so he was arrested for carrying a pistol.

The case came up in City Court, and the judge gave Mr. Seymore sixty days in jail! I was shocked, so, of course, I appealed the matter to the Criminal Court, where it was set in Judge Joseph McCartie's court. McCartie was a tough and sometimes overbearing personality, but he was street-wise.

Fortunately, Judge McCartie understood this situation, and wasn't about to put this old-timer in jail, but he wanted to get Mr. Seymore's attention. The judge said, "The fine is five hundred dollars, which is due thirty days from now; I'm not going to put you in jail." Mr. Seymore was relieved and pleased.

Several weeks later, I received a telephone call from his eighty-year-old girlfriend. She said, "Seymore just had a heart attack!" She added, "But, as the ambulance people were carrying him off, he raised his head, and hollered to me, 'DON'T FORGET TO TAKE THE FINE MONEY TO THE LAWYER!'"

Oops!!!!

Years ago, the Supreme Court of Tennessee established the Board of Professional Responsibility, a group of lawyers to monitor complaints against lawyers in the state to evaluate said complaints, and, if necessary, to take action against offenders, etc.

The director of the board was, and is, Lance Bracey, and second in authority was, and is, Ms. Laura Chastain. They discharge their duties with fairness, not only to the complainants, but also to the alleged offenders.

A few years ago, my wife and I were having dinner at the buffet in the Horseshoe Casino (Tunica, Mississippi) just a few miles from Memphis. I saw my friend, lawyer Ted Hanson, and Larry Finch, former basketball coach at Memphis State, also dining with a group of five or six people at a large table. I got up and went over to their table, and said, "Hi, Ted, how are you doing?"

Ted replied, "Hi, Manuel, what are you doing here?" Knowing Ted appreciates a good joke, I said, "I'm here spending my clients' trust funds." Smiling broadly and pointing, Ted replied, "Let me introduce you to Laura Chastain!" Stunned, I groped for a proper retort, and responded, "Oh, it's only a small one, thirty or forty thousand dollars!" Everyone but me broke out in loud laughter.

I am told that Ms. Chastain tells that story as an opening joke whenever she conducts an ethics seminar.

Lawyers Come First!

I get very disturbed when lawyers fail or refuse to return telephone calls. Generally, most lawyers do return calls; but in recent times, there have been too many (men and women) who have this bad habit.

Not long ago, after several telephone calls not returned, I finally reached this young lawyer. I said to him, "Listen, kid, you should always return telephone calls for two reasons!"

He said, "What are they?" I replied, "First, you might make some money; but second, and more important, lawyers are the only friends lawyers have!"

Advice to the Judge!

About six or seven years ago, I was before Judge Joe McCartie in Criminal Court with a client who was seeking suspension of sentence (probation) for a felony matter. My client, a plumber and a first offender, did a stupid thing by allowing himself to be involved, etc. Nevertheless, Judge McCartie was not easy in granting probation, and getting probation was not a "slam-dunk," as he always found reasons to deny the application.

During the hearing, in addition to my client, we presented six witnesses who spoke up for my client's good behavior, etc. The judge asked each of them if my client had told them what he did, and why he did it. Each witness said no. That seemed to bother Judge McCartie, as he displayed his displeasure with the negative responses.

As I was making my closing argument and seeking probation, Judge McCartie interrupted me, and talked about the failure of my client to tell the witnesses about what he did. As I stood there, I pointed to the judge and said, "Judge, let me give you some advice!"

"What!" shouted the judge, "I'm seventy years old!"

"I'm almost there," I replied.

"All right, what is it?" he asked grudgingly.

Like the oracle at Delphi, I said, "An old politician told me once that when one ever gets in trouble his real friends don't care to know why or the details, but your enemies do!" The silence was deafening. After probation was granted, the judge called me to the bench, and said quietly, "Who was that politician?"

That's Gratitude!

A very disgruntled woman burst into this lawyer's office one day, and, after passing by the secretary's desk, confronted her lawyer of many years, shouting, "You are a cheat, you have kept me hanging for months, not returning my many telephone calls. AND you got rich on my case alone!"

"That's gratitude for you," said the lawyer, "and right after I named my new yacht after you!"

Manuel P. Scarmoutsos

Judge Bailey Brown

Judge Brown served with distinction for many years as a trial judge in the U.S. District Court in Memphis. He was able, colorful, and funny at times, and most lawyers enjoyed their practice before him. He had a great sense of humor.

About twenty or thirty years ago I represented a man from out of town named Silver. I doubt if that was his real name, since he had many "A/K/As." He was charged with stealing and transporting a Lincoln automobile across state lines. We had a plausible defense, but it was an uphill battle. The trial lasted just short of a full day, but the jury deliberated for almost a day and half before returning a verdict of guilty. Sentencing took place a month later.

At the sentencing hearing, Judge Brown asked me if I had anything to say. Probation was out of the question because the defendant had a "rap sheet" of several pages with non-violent crimes.

Searching for something good to say, I told Judge Brown, "I ask that you be lenient, Judge, since it was obviously a close case since the jury was out for a day and a half." Leaning forward from the bench, Judge Brown explained, *"Yeah, I know it. They should have come back in FIVE minutes!"*

Now That's Convincing!

Years ago, I represented a former football player at Memphis State who was charged with attempted rape. It was a bitter trial with twenty-nine witnesses for the state and only one for the defense (the defendant).

The trial lasted four full days. During the third day, my client tapped me on the shoulder and said, "Hey, Manuel, the more you talk, the more I believe I didn't do it!"

(p.s. The trial ended with a hung jury 9-3 for acquittal.)

* * *

This same person was a suspect in the burglary of a hardware store in the Memphis State area. According to the owner of the store, a young man came in on a Saturday morning and asked to buy a crowbar. Asked if he wanted anything else, he said, "Yes, I need some rope."

"How much? asked the owner. Looking up to the ceiling of the store, the young man said, "About from the ceiling to the floor." When the owner opened his store on Monday morning, he found a piece of rope hanging from the ceiling to the floor, and his cash register broken and empty!

Manuel P. Scarmoutsos

Look Who's Coming To Dinner?

The *voir dire* examination (picking a jury) is a critical part in the beginning of a jury case. The answers received from a prospective jury may, in some instances, make the difference in whether the man or woman is accepted.

Several years ago, I represented a defendant in a serious civil case in Judge Irving Strauch's Circuit Court, Division IV. Judge Strauch, a serious, no-nonsense judge, tolerated little humor in the courtroom. He was all business, but a good person.

As usual, the attorney for the plaintiff questioned the prospective jury, and, if satisfied, accepted the jury, which happened in this case. It was now my turn.

There was one woman on the jury. I noted that the plaintiff's attorney, Stanley Fink, a friend of mine, never asked the woman about her husband, his occupation, etc. This woman's name was Ms. Louise McRae, the wife of federal judge Robert McRae. I did not know her at that time. Here's how the questioning went:

MPS: "Ms. McRae, is there a Mr. McRae?" (This is the polite way to see if she is still married, divorced, or widowed.)

SHE: "Yes."

MPS: "Is he employed, and if so, by whom?"

SHE: "Yes, by the federal government." (Well, the bell rang loud!)

MPS: "That wouldn't be the U.S. District for the Western District of Tennessee?"

SHE: "I'm sorry to say that's him." (Everyone broke in laughter with her, the loudest.)

MPS: "Ms. McRae, when you and your husband are having dinner, do you discuss the law and law issues?"

SHE: "Oh, no, I just listen."

MPS: "You are a good lawyer's wife." (More laughter by all, including her)

SHE: "And besides, he usually talked about the lawyers." (Laughter)

MPS: After a long pause, "Well, you know, we have had HIM for dinner, too!"

The jury practically exploded with laughter, and Ms. McRae was the loudest. We left her on the jury, she became the foreperson, and WE GOT THE VERDICT!!!!

Chancellor Charles Rond

Pirates and Thieves

Lawyer James Cox and lawyer Palmer Miller had a case before Chancellor Rond one time where a used car salesman was suing a defendant. Before ruling, Chancellor Rond announced to the lawyer as follows, "The court will take judicial notice that used car salesmen are direct descendants of pirates and horse thieves!"

UNFROCKED AND UNASHAMED

The following article was written by my good friend, David Wade, who recently served as president of the Memphis Bar Association. This was about a humorous criminal trial about twenty years ago that appeared in the bar newsletter:

My Most Amusing Moment in Court

BY DAVID WADE

The funniest incident I have seen in court did not involve me personally. It involved two of the best-humored attorneys who have practiced at the Memphis bar, Wayne G. Emmons and Manuel P. Scarmoutsos. Wayne was representing the state of Tennessee in a hard-fought criminal case, with Manny holding forth for the defense.

At the conclusion of the case, these two sizable members of the bar prepared for their final arguments. General Emmons, towering over the jury, launched into one of his finest dissertations on motherhood, country, and apple pie. With the skill of a good Southern preacher, he molded the jury into a single body that appeared certain to vote "guilty as charged." His eloquent homespun style, highlighted with easygoing good humor, created a difficult obstacle for Manny to overcome if he were to win the case.

Manuel Scarmoutsos, however, is a man equal to the task. Summoning all of his southern Mediterranean powers of persuasion, using his most engaging smile, and swaying the jury with his ever winsome personality, he implored them "not to fall victim to General Emmon's 'Roger Miller'-style approach to argument."

As he sat down, it was clear that Manny had broken Wayne's spell over the twelve tried and true citizens. The burden was on the state. Emmons rose out of his chair and surveyed the jury. Then he closed the case: "Ladies and gentlemen, I don't know what Mr. Scarmoutous means by 'Roger Miller'-style approach, but if his client isn't guilty, then God didn't make little green apples and it don't rain in Indianapolis in the summertime!"

Lawyers who frequented the old criminal courts in those days often talk when they meet of the immortal voices that echoed in those now silent chambers. And when closing arguments are discussed, you can be sure that the great battle of these two giants is the first to be recounted.

**Attorneys Wayne Emmons
and Manuel Scarmoutsos
"Memorable Moments"**

Manuel P. Scarmoutsos

Courts I Have Appeared in September 1960–June 2003

TENNESSEE:
Shelby County (Memphis) • Lauderdale County (Ripley)
Hardeman County (Bolivar) • Giles County (Pulaski)
Davidson County (Nashville) • McNairy County (Selmer)
Fayette County (Somerville) • Knox County (Knoxville)
Tipton County (Covington) • White County (Sparta)
Dyer County (Dyersburg) • Rutherford County (Murfreesboro)
Lawrence County (Lawrenceburg) • Obion County (Union City)
Chester County (Henderson) • Benton County (Camden)

OTHER STATES:
Columbia, Missouri • Desoto County, Mississippi (Hernando) • Oxford, Mississippi • Cape Girardeau, Missouri • Tupelo, Mississippi • Charleston, Misssissippi • Holly Springs, Misssissippi • Ponotoc, Misssissippi • Little Rock, Arkansas • Petersburg, Indiana • New Britain, Connecticut • Zenia, Ohio • Pimeville, Kentucky • Mayfield, Kentucky • Dallas, Texas • Monticello, Kentucky • Carthage, Texas • West Memphis, Arkansas • Blytheville, Arkansas

FEDERAL COURT:
U.S. Supreme Court (Washington, D.C.)
6th Circuit Court of Appeals (Cincinnati, Ohio)

DISTRICT COURTS:
Memphis, Tennessee
Nashville, Tennessee
St. Louis, Missouri
Aberdeen, Mississippi
Brooklyn, New York

About the Author

I was born, at a very early age, on September 1, 1929, in Corning, a small city in western upstate New York. My parents were Peter and Eve Scarmoutsos, both immigrants from Koupia and Niata, two small villages near Sparta.

My father owned and operated a candy, ice cream, and light lunch store in Corning for about thirty years until he passed away in March 1953. Growing up in Corning (population 18,000) was a wonderful experience. Our life centered around the store, "Crystal Confectionery," which was located in the middle of downtown. The store's nickname was "Pete's" and that was what everybody called it. Open seven days a week, it was a true family operation, my father, sisters, (later cousins), and I.

We had a big adult clientele, and many students from the three area high schools. My father ran it with a "big fist" with three simple rules for the students: no loitering, no standing at the booths, and everyone had to order something, if only a ten-cent coke. There was an unwritten rule among the students. "If you have not been thrown out of 'Pete's' at least once, you have not made the grade!"

I have two older sisters, Mrs. Stella Chigounis of Cherry Hill, New Jersey, and Mrs. Catherine Bashakes of Royal

Oak, Michigan. A third sister, Artemis, died not long after birth. My mother passed away in June 1935, when I was only five years old, and I have always regretted missing the love and care of a mother.

I attended and graduated from Corning Free Academy in June 1947, and to this day I have contact with many of my classmates, who made school great for me. Few would believe that I never had a date in high school. Because though I played football, basketball, and track, I was always working in the store! However, I made up for it in college.

My father was a great man and a patriot. He came to America in the early 1920s, and began working for a Greek friend in Leroy, New York, learning the confectionery business as did hundreds of Greek immigrants in those days in upstate New York. After saving his money, he moved to Corning and opened the Crystal Confectionery, "crystal" because Corning was heavy involved in the production of glass products. He learned to speak English well, and was a successful businessman, a member of Rotary, civic leader, and a member of the Citizens' Committee on the Hoover Report. In 1943, a group of city leaders encouraged him to run for mayor of Corning. Though he did not win, it was a grand tribute, since I believe he was one of the first immigrants from Greece to run for mayor of an American city. Second out of four wasn't bad!! When World War II broke out, my father joined the National Guard (at age 51), and participated in weekly drills at the local Armory. He died on March 18, 1953. Stern, immobile at times, but generous and fair. He was a grand person. I think of him often.

From 1947 to 1949, I attended Genessee Junior College (Lima, New York) where I was active in football, basketball, soccer, and track. Our basketball team was outstanding, 55-15 in two years was a proud record. From 1949 to January 1952, I transferred to State University of New York at Geneseo (SUNY), and was also active in basketball and soccer. I was never an outstanding athlete, but good enough to make the college teams.

I recall, vividly, finishing college (B.S. Education) on a Friday in January 1952, and driving all night to Cleveland, Ohio, to join the Marine Corps and the OCC (Officer Candidate Class). I never saw my father cry except for the time he pinned my 2nd Lieutenant bars on me in Quantico, Virginia, when his eyes were filled with proud tears.

After Quantico, I spent four months at Camp Lejune, North Carolina, when I received my orders for Korea. Coming home for the customary two weeks' leave, tragedy struck our family as my father suddenly died at the age of only 61. The Corps gave me an extension of leave, two more weeks so I could handle affairs at the store. I spent all that time making chocolate rabbits, eggs, and candies, as the Easter holiday season was only a few weeks away.

Korea was an experience, both good and bad. Serving with the historic 1st Marine Division was a proud time that I will cherish forever. Shortly after the cease fire (July 26, 1953), I was ordered on special assignment as the liaison officer with the Greek Expeditionary Forces until I finished my tour in March 1954. That was tough duty as we were on the DMZ, but a memorable experience. At least my Greek improved a great deal, since except for ten enlisted men under my command, no one of the fifteen hundred troops spoke English.

After coming home, it was too late to enter law school for the fall, so I had to wait until the fall of 1955 to enter Georgetown Law School. My high school principal, Wilbur T. Miller, whom we affectionately called "Baldy," asked me to teach seventh and eighth graders at my former high school (CFA). Indeed, that was a great experience, because here I was on the faculty where my colleagues were many of those who had taught me only a few years before. They were very kind to me.

In the early summer of 1955, a friend of mine from Corning, Peter Bacalles, was getting married to a young lady in Memphis, Tennessee. He asked me to attend since the only person able to make the trip was his cousin and best man, Nick Bacalles. Who said that long distance relationships don't work! Well, it did in our case, because at the wedding reception I met Georgia Avgeris on June 6, 1955, and we became engaged on August 15, 1955, and married on December 25, 1955! She has been my wife, companion, and friend ever since.

After one year at Georgetown Law School, we took a break and lived in Rochester, New York, for a year. Then we moved to Memphis in February 1957, and I entered night law school at Southern Law University. Working days and going to school at night was a grind, but I was determined to attain my goal, and I earned my L.L.B. in late 1959. After passing the bar examination I began practicing law in Memphis in the summer of 1960, and have been doing so to the present time.

Georgia and I were blessed with three children, Peter, Eve, and Andrew. Peter is a manufacturer's rep with The Roma Corporation, and presently lives in Birmingham. Eve is married to George Pappas and they reside in Atlanta. They have given us two beautiful grandsons, John and Emanuel Andrew.

The greatest tragedy in our lives was when Andrew (age 29) was killed in a house fire in Memphis in October 2000. All of us were devastated as this tested our faith. I am told that one never really gets over the loss of a child, and that all we can do is go forward. We are doing the best we can. We have set up a scholarship fund in Andrew's name, and we are in hope that certain proceeds from the sale of this book will be added to that fund as a living memorial.

After we moved to Memphis in 1957, Georgia and I became heavily involved in many aspects of our local parish, Annunciation Greek Orthodox Church, including the choir, Sunday school, and G.O.Y.A. (Greek Orthodox Youth of America), a young adult organization of the Church that sponsors many charitable and religious programs. In 1960, I was elected national chairman.

In the late '90s I became more active in the Order of A.H.E.P.A. (American Hellenic Education Progressive Association), a national fraternity of men with a women's auxiliary dedicated to charitable deeds, scholarship, disaster relief, etc. I have been honored to serve several national offices since then to the present time. As in G.O.Y.A., Georgia and I have made many lasting friendships with men and women throughout the nation through A.H.E.P.A. that we cherish and enjoy even today.

Practicing law in Memphis these past forty-three years has been mostly a plus for me. We have made many wonderful friends among the judges and lawyers in this community, including some clients.

Memphis has been good to me and my family. I hope this book is a small contribution in return.

—Manuel P. Scarmoutsos

Bonus Comment

The Greek philosopher Plato once said, "The best defense against insanity is humor...." No, wait. Maybe that was attorney Manuel P. Scarmoutsos. Anyway, regardless of who said it, it's an absolute truth. Humor is good for what ails the human condition. It helps us heal while nourishing the soul with the brightness of smiles and laughter. The author has made a longitudinal study of the lighter side of the law and litigation for us to read and enjoy. Have fun!

About the illustrator

John R. "Jack" Cassady is a cartoonist, humorous illustrator and designer. His work has appeared in hundreds of publications, on television, and on the Internet. His studio is in the foothills of the North Carolina Smoky Mountains, where he lives with his wife, dogs, cats, and forest critters. Cassady is a member of the National Cartoonists Society and the Graphic Artists Guild.

About the cover

The seat of Western Civilization can be found in Ancient Greece and Rome. Art, a system of government, and the law are only a few of the many major contributions given to us by these incredible cultures.

The unfrocked Lady Justice is based on the Greek goddess Themis. A regal vaudevillian-like attorney, who amazingly resembles our author, protects her from the prying eyes of the public. He sports the footwear of choice for lawyers throughout the ages, wingtip shoes.